Poems
Of
Praise

By
Rosalie Holder

Dedication

This book of poems is dedicated to my mother, who always encouraged me and told me to never give up.

And to the Lord who gave me the gift and desire to write.

Acknowledgments

I would like to thank my family for their love and support.

Thank you to my church family, Pastor Eddie Sneed and Sister Virginia Sneed for their encouragement. As well as the entire St. Luke, AME family who have always given me the chance to share my poems.

And to Minister Jon and Doctor Naima Johnston Bush who coordinated the publishing process.

Tell Old Satan

Open the door
Tell Old Satan
To get stepping,
Don't come back here,
Anymore

Just ask him once and don't repeat it
Twice, Jesus is the head of my life!

If he don't listen to what you say,
Turn to Jesus
He will show you the way

Open your heart
Clear your mind
Tell Old Satan to walk behind

As long as we got Jesus on our side,
Walk with your head up high
Beaming with spiritual pride

Walk A Little Slower Daddy
On The Occasion of Father's Day
Dedicated to all the Daddies that Lead by Example

Walk a little slower daddy,
Said a child so small

I'm following in your footsteps
And I don't want to fall

Sometimes your steps are very fast,
Sometimes they are hard to see
So walk a little slower Daddy,
For you are leading me

Someday when I am all grown up,
You're what I want to be

Then I will have a little child
Who will want to follow me

And I would want to lead just so
And know that I was true

So walk a little slower daddy,
For I must follow you

Get On Board

How would you like to take a ride?
There is no need for pride

God is the engineer
Jesus is the Conductor

You don't need a ticket just
Get On Board

Lay back and relax
This ride is like no other

We are all Sisters and Brothers
Can you see yourself going down the track

With Jesus at your back
What a sight it would be

For the world to see
We are riding happy and carefree,

So don't get lost or go astray
The Holy Train will come back every day

Take Time

Take time to pray... Not only for yourself, but for others as well

Take time for friends… If it's only to talk, laugh, joke or take a walk

Take time for work… You can make it a success, just do your best

Take time to think ... Of others, God gave you the power to glow like a beautiful flower

Take time to read … The Bible and learn about our Lord and Savior, Jesus Christ

Take time to laugh… It's a sound God loves to hear, your heart is full of good cheer

Take time to love … One another, It's a sacrament of life

Take time to dream… Of all the wonderful things God has bestowed on you

Take time to play… Have fun in every kind of way, and you will have a good day

Take time to worship… It's the highway to the kingdom of heaven

God's House

On your way to God's House
These are the sights you will see,
Twelve Gates to the city

Three Gates in the East
Three Gates in the West
Three Gates in the North
Three Gates in the South
The streets are paved with gold

Everywhere you go there is a beautiful soul,
With a story about Jesus to be told

This is a city that's full of life
Oh, what a delight
To get your wings that shine so bright

There is no sickness
No pain
No crying
No shame
So who are we to complain?

It is so peaceful there
Angels are glowing everywhere

When I get to God's House
I will be free
To meet The Man who created me

Time Is Winding Down

The Lord is watching you
He knows just what you are going to do
Don't try to hide
Hold your head
Walk with pride
For the Lord is on your side

Time is winding down
Don't walk around
All your life with a frown
Don't you want to go to Heaven,
To get your crown?

I don't know about you
But I do!
What a joy it would be
For my Jesus and me

How would you like to see him face to face?
All you need is faith and grace to win Jesus' race

For He sits high and He looks low
No matter where you go

Time Is Winding Down
I don't know about you
But I am heaven bound

Don't Give Up

Let Jesus take over
It's like finding a four leaf clover

Your luck will change for the best
Turn to Jesus he will do the rest

Don't let Satan get in your head
he will have you in his spell
And your soul will go to hell

Turn to Jesus
He knows just what to do
Satan will destroy your soul
Jesus will pick you up and make you whole

Don't give up
Jesus has something special for you

Satan is full of greed and sin
But if you want to win ask Jesus to come in

Jesus is full of eternal life and love
It's like flying on the wings
Of a beautiful white dove

The only thing Satan has for you is fire and
brimstone

So don't give up'
Take a drink from Jesus holy cup

St. Luke's Kids

They are so precious to us
I'm not bragging it's a fact

When they sing for the Lord
There's no holding back
Our little Angels right here on earth
With a smile on their face with elegance and grace

Their voices are as pure as can be
When you hear them sing
You will see

Travis on the drums
He knows how to make them hum

Neisha has a voice so sweet and pure
She belongs to St. Luke for sure

Angela on the piano playing a song
Just follow her lead and you won't go wrong
Just to name a few

Without our Saint Luke's Kids
What would we do?

A Blessing Such As You

In all the things you say and do
I see the very heart of you
Your joy, your caring
Your love, your sharing

Reaching out
Touching a life
Bringing freedom
From one's strife
Showing someone
That you care
When the burden seems
Too hard to bear

In ways so gentle
Ways so kind
To others you bring
Peace of mind
Your prayers and thoughts
Mean so much
Do you realize the lives you touch?

I see your soul
Your spirit too
Such a beautiful reflection
Of God in you

I'm forever grateful
He chose to send
A blessing such as you

Friendship Flowers

Life is like a garden
Friendship is like a flower
That blooms and grow in beauty
With the sunshine and the shower

Lovely are the blossoms
That are tended with great care
By those who work unselfishly
To make the place more fair

Like the garden blossoms
Friendship flowers grow more sweet
When watched and tended carefully
By those we know and meet

If the seed of friendship
God planted deep and true
Is watched with understanding
Friendship flowers will bloom for you

Jesus Still Lives

For in my mind
I see a vision of Him all the time
Within my heart I know
He breathes with grace and ease

I am going to do all His will
Because I know Jesus still lives

Has Jesus ever failed you yet?

Jesus can see you
He knows just what you are going to do

Remember when Jesus died on the cross
Our souls were not lost

One of the Ten Commandments says,
"Thou shall not kill"
That's the reason our Jesus still lives

The Old Rugged Cross

There was a Man no one could understand
They treated Him mean and cruel
And did not obey His Father's Golden Rule

He walked the earth with holy grace
To see His people face to face

He talked to the sinners and thieves too
They did not know what to do

His name is Jesus this is true
He died on the rugged old cross
For me and you

My God, My God

His blessing is what I seek

My God, My God, He is so sweet

He can make the seasons change

Turn a sunny day into rain

Bring the moon out at night

Turn the morning into light

He can heal the sick and raise the dead

My God, My God

His Blood was red

The Garden

I go to the garden to speak
With my Lord
To tell my troubles too

And while I am there
He's also praying for you

So when I leave the garden
I am happy as can be
I know my Lord Jesus Christ
Is watching over thee

God's Ears

From your mouth to God's Ears
We should never have any fears

For God is with us all the time
That lets me know

We are doing just fine
So keep the faith day by day

God will bless you in every way

Jesus Will Always Pull You Through

Everyday that you live
That's a reason to forgive
No matter what they do to you
Remember Jesus will always pull you through

Open your heart, your soul, your mind
Let Jesus come in
You will be fine

All the things that we do
Jesus is always watching over you

He will pour you out a blessing
For this is true

Jesus will always pull you through

He

He gives hope where there is none
He gives life when our candle burns short

He gives peace when our world is in turmoil
He gives strength when we are weak

He loves us when no one cares
He washes us clean as snow

He is a gift more precious than diamonds or gold
He is a gift of true love, joy, peace
And life beyond the grave

He is our Lord and Savior Jesus Christ

They Hung Him High

His blood ran red
With a crown of thorns on His head

Jesus didn't lay
In the tomb for long

God sent Him back
Twice as strong

Jesus walks the earth everyday
Help poor sinners along the way

Do you know why?
They Hung Him High!

Satan Is A Liar

Don't believe what he says
he will have you doing his way

he lives in brimstone and in fire
So now you know

Satan is a liar

You can't trust him day or night
Turn to God for eternal life

His Amazing Grace

Have you ever been baptized and did not realize
Something came over you
Your soul got happy
You could not be still
Oh, Lord what a thrill!

Your heart was full of joy
Like a child with a brand new toy
Your feet was moving all over the place
One of these days we will look upon His face

Then we will know
That we have won the race
Thank God for His Amazing Grace

Bless The Children

Bless the children of the world
It doesn't matter if it's a boy or a girl

Whether they are big or small
Short or tall

Remember God made them all

By using dirt from lands
He formed us with His mighty hands

His image is plain to see
God created you and me

Give In

devil you may as well give in
With God's children you can't win

devil you may be big, bad and bold
Our God has a heart of gold

devil you will never take our soul

Let me tell you about our God
He is mighty, good and strong
When someone like you devil comes along

God will pick us up and we do no wrong
There's no way our God will let you win
devil you must give in

Communion

The wine is for the blood
He shed way back on Calvary
It's because He died for you and me

The bread is for eternal life
Before and beyond the grave
Thank God almighty from above
That my soul is saved

So remember when you take Communion
You are not taking it for me
You are taking it for a man named Jesus
Who died on Calvary

I Love The Lord

He is so good to me
My soul is happy and free

I can call on Him day or night
And everything will be alright

Whenever I need Him
He is there
With open arms because He cares

He will go out of His way
To make my day

I love the Lord
What more can I say

He Gave Me

God has done amazing things for me
He gave me eyes so I can see

He gave me ears so I can hear
There is no reason for me to fear

He gave me a mouth so I can talk
And two legs so I can walk

He gave me hands so I can write
During the day or by night

He gave me wisdom
To know right from wrong
I can talk about God all day long

Adam and Eve

They were in the Garden all alone
Eve was weak and Adam was strong

Then the devil showed his face
Oh my God what a disgrace
Everything went wild in that place

Now you see how the devil can trick you
Making you believe what God said is not true

Bless This House

Bless this house, O Lord we pray
Make it safe by night and day

Bless these walls so firm and stout
Keeping want and trouble out

Bless the roof and chimney tall
Let thy peace lay over all

Bless the door that it may open forever more

Bless these windows shinning bright
Letting in God's heavenly light

Bless the people who dwell within
Keep them pure and free from sin

Dining With God

Dining with God
It is a pleasure
Better than a golden treasure

Can you see God sitting at the head of your table
Reared back looking at the cable

This is the twenty first century as you know
Please don't act up or put on a show
God has many places He must go

Treat Him sweet and do be kind
God will never leave you behind

Call on God

You can't fight the devil by yourself
You can call on God for some help

And if the devil tries to attack
God will be there to watch your back

The devil is tricky this you know
For God has already told you so

The devil can sneak and hide
Without any pride

So call on God
To be your guide

Can't Nobody Do Me Like Jesus

He woke me up this morning
In my right mind
He started me on my way
Lord thank you for a brand new day

Bless His Holy Name
He is in heaven's Hall of Fame
He's the one who gives me strength when I am
weak
Picks me up when I fall

Glory be to God
He is my all and all
He's worthy to be praised
He died for my sins
And on the third day
He rose from the dead

With two little fish
Five loaves of bread
A multitude my Savior fed

His name is Jesus
Whenever you pray
Remember there is a way
No matter what you are going through
He can pick you up and turn you around
Plant your feet on solid ground

God's Unchanging Hand

Hold on to God's unchanging hand
Don't let go
Because if you do
The devil will be there to convince you

Don't let the devil in your life
He will destroy your soul
Have you doing things beyond your control

Why do wrong?
When you can do right
The devil loves to see you
Fuss and fight

So hold on to God's Unchanging hand
He's the man with a mighty plan

My Prayer

I pray that this old world
Can become as one
When everybody can laugh
Have some fun

No more fighting or using a gun
We can put the devil on the run

No more crying
No more dying
And most of all
No more lying

We need to love one another
Like a sister or a brother

I am only human
It is plain to see

Thank God Almighty
That He created me

Jesus

He has a gentle touch
He cares for His people so much

He gives good advice
Sometimes He has to repeat Himself twice

His work is very hard each and every day
Listen to what Jesus has to say

He knows exactly what to do
To keep the devil away from you

Jesus Is The Way

Jesus is the way
Whenever you kneel down and pray

He's the one and only
Savior Jesus Christ
He is the one who gave you life

Do you know this Man
He is always willing
To give you a helping hand

I have tried Him and I know
Because He showed me
The right way to go

He brought me
A mighty long way
I am a living witness
For Him today

Thank God I can say
Jesus is the way!

A Friend
For Carolyn

Carolyn was a friend to one and all
You just pick up the phone
And give her a call

When asked would you sing a solo
On our program
Even if she was there
To enjoy the service
All you had to do was ask
And she would sing

Her favorite song
Thank you Lord
Whenever you heard her sing
She would bring tears to your eyes
Joy to your heart
And peace to your soul

She had a voice of gold
Now she's with the angels
Singing in God's Holy Choir
We miss you
Had a lot of fun

This poem is dedicated to you
Carolyn Brazelton

Pastor

You are a kind warm hearted person
Every time I see you working
You are always on the go

You greet me with a hug
And with a smile

When you walk with pep
In your step
Willing to give everybody some help
Your personality just beams
All over the place
With style and grace

You will never be alone
God Almighty
Is always on the throne
When I bring you candy
Your face just lights up
And that makes my day in everyway

You are, a Man of God
It's plain to see
Without you here
In St. Luke where would we be?

His Tear Strains

Sometimes I feel His pains
The Lord left me with
His tear strains

Upon the cross is where He died
With blood running out of His side
So what did the people gain
Nothing but
His tear strains

So don't you worry
Don't you fret
He has never failed you yet

So don't move over
In the right lane
Worship the Lord
And His tear strains

Give Us Strength

If Satan's way we seek to go
Lord give us strength to tell him no
Don't let our souls be led astray
Please give us strength
For one more day

And if we fall along the way
Then lift us up
Oh Lord we pray

For Satan's strong
Your grace we need
When Satan makes
Our spirits bleed

Give us strength
Oh Lord we pray
To fight this demon day by day

Satan's working over time
Trying his best to change our mind
But if you help us Lord
We know his evil seed
Will never grow

For you are mightier
Then the sword
We have chosen
You to be our Lord

So give us strength
Oh, Lord we pray
By standing in the devil's way

A Slice Of The Devil's Pie

Have you ever had the urge to say or do something
And in your heart you know that it was wrong
But you did it anyway?
You should have been strong
Instead you chose to take, a slice of the devil's pie
Don't let the demon of sin get his hooks
Into your skin, he is not your friend

The devil is full of hate, greed, rage, evil and lies
Why would you want a slice of devil's pie?
Now that you know what's in the pie
Turn to God and tell the devil bye bye

Give God's angel food cake a try
It is filed with love, hope, faith, blessing, praise and
eternal life

You can talk and walk, hold your head up high
Look at God's great big beautiful sky
You should have no questions on who, what, where
or why, God has no reason to tell you a lie

Put some of God's angel food cake
On your plate remember God created
The heavens and the earth

How would you like to go through
Those pearly gates
Where the streets are paved with gold
And your soul will never grow old

Thank You Lord

Tomorrow is not promised to us
So I shall not delay
I want to say
Thank You Lord
For yesterday

This is what we should do
Not just say don't wait it might be to late
Stand up and preach
Or kneel down and pray
Say thank you Lord for yesterday

He knows how much you can stand
So get up
Give the Lord a great big hand
Thank Him
For giving you another day

Please don't forget to say
Thank You Lord
For yesterday

Sister Rosalie Holder

Rosalie Holder shares from her beautiful heart, poems of praise and adoration that celebrate faith, hope and love.

She is a member of St. Luke AME, Church in Nashville, TN where she is affectionately known as Sister Rose. She works tirelessly in ministry work and has been writing her entire life.

This book of poems is a testament of years of work that admonishes the believer to be encouraged, stay focused on the Lord, to serve and most importantly to love.

Sister Rose is blessed to be a Christian and to be in service to the Lord through her writing and volunteer work.